DISCOVERING THE UNITED STATES

# West Virginia

BY DAVID J. CLARKE

An Imprint of Abdo Publishing
abdobooks.com

**abdobooks.com**



Printed in China.
052024
092024

Cover Photo: Sean Pavone/Shutterstock Images
Interior Photos: Science Source/Photo Researchers History/Archive Photos/Getty Images, 4–5; Ivy Close Images/Alamy, 7; Bonnie Taylor Barry/Shutterstock Images, 8 (top left); iStockphoto, 8 (top right), 14; Shutterstock Images, 8 (bottom left), 23, 28 (top right); Nathan A. Shepard/Shutterstock Images, 8 (bottom right); Zack Frank/Shutterstock Images, 10; Malachi Jacobs/Shutterstock Images, 12–13, 18; Image Professionals GmbH/Foodcollection/Getty Images, 17; Sean Pavone/Shutterstock Images, 20–21, 28 (bottom); Gareth McCormack/Alamy, 25; Dynamic Photography/Shutterstock Images, 26; Red Line Editorial, 28 (top left), 29 (top); Jon Bilous/Shutterstock Images, 29 (bottom)

Editor: Haley Williams
Series Designer: Katharine Hale

**Library of Congress Control Number: 2023949379**

**Publisher's Cataloging-in-Publication Data**

Names: Clarke, David J., author.
Title: West Virginia / by David J. Clarke
Description: Minneapolis, Minnesota: Abdo Publishing, 2025 | Series: Discovering the United States | Includes online resources and index.
Identifiers: ISBN 9781098294205 (lib. bdg.) | ISBN 9798384913474 (ebook)
Subjects: LCSH: U.S. states--Juvenile literature. | West Virginia--History--Juvenile literature. | Southeastern States--Juvenile literature. | Physical geography--United States--Juvenile literature.
Classification: DDC 973--dc23

All population data taken from:
"Estimates of Population by Sex, Race, and Hispanic Origin: April 1, 2020 to July 1, 2022." *US Census Bureau, Population Division*, June 2023, census.gov.

# CONTENTS

John Brown was known for his commitment to freedom.

# CHAPTER 1

# John Brown's Raid

In 1859, the United States was divided over slavery. Southern states wanted to keep slavery legal. Northern states wanted to end it. A man named John Brown arrived in what is now West Virginia on July 3, 1859. Brown wanted to end slavery.

On the night of October 16, 1859, Brown and 21 other men took over the US **armory** in Harpers Ferry. Brown's plan was to free enslaved people in the area. He would give them guns and form an army. That army would then move south to free more enslaved people.

However, Brown's plan didn't work. The townspeople of Harpers Ferry fought Brown and his men. Then the US Army arrived in the town. It surrounded Brown's men. By October 19, Brown's **rebellion** was over.

Although his plan failed, many people believed Brown was a hero. His actions helped spark the start of the American Civil War (1861–1865). The war ended slavery in the

US forces attacked the armory where Brown and his men hid.

United States. Today, many tourists go to West Virginia to visit Harpers Ferry. There, they can see the armory. They can also read about John Brown's failed rebellion.

## West Virginia Facts

**DATE OF STATEHOOD**
June 20, 1863

**CAPITAL**
Charleston

**POPULATION**
1,775,156

**AREA**
24,230 square miles
(62,775 sq km)

STATE BIRD

Northern cardinal

STATE TREE

Sugar maple

STATE FLOWER

Rhododendron

STATE AMPHIBIAN

Red salamander

Each US state has a different population, size, and capital city. States also have state symbols.

# West Virginia's Land

West Virginia is in the US region called the South. Virginia borders West Virginia to the southeast. To the northeast are Maryland

and Pennsylvania. Ohio sits on the western border of West Virginia. And Kentucky is to the southwest.

Most of West Virginia's land is covered by mountains. The Appalachian Mountains run through the state. West Virginia is also home to large forests. Common trees in the state include ash, sugar maple, and white pine.

## The Split

West Virginia was originally part of Virginia. During the American Civil War, Virginia voted to split from the United States. But the people in the western part of the state wanted to stay in the nation. They decided to start their own **territory**. In 1863, the United States added West Virginia as its thirty-fifth state.

Harpers Ferry sits on the edge of the Potomac River.

Several major rivers run through West Virginia. They include the New River, the Ohio River, and the Potomac River. Fish such as bass, trout, and catfish swim in the state's rivers.

## West Virginia's Climate

West Virginia has four seasons. Winters are snowy in the mountains. Summers in the state are warm and **humid**. Fall and spring are usually mild. Floods are common during the spring. The state is also known for its severe summer thunderstorms.

### Further Evidence

Look at the website below. Does it give any new evidence to support Chapter One?

**Harpers Ferry National Historical Park**

abdocorelibrary.com/discovering-west-virginia

Many American Indian peoples in West Virginia gather to celebrate their cultures.

# The People of West Virginia

American Indians have lived in West Virginia for more than 14,000 years. One nation that once lived in the state were the Shawnee. The Shawnee hunted, fished, and farmed. They also built homes out of wood. These are known as wigwams.

West Virginia's flag features a wreath of rhododendrons. The rhododendron is the state flower.

Other nations in West Virginia include the Delaware, the Cherokee, the Saponi, and the Mingo. French fur traders began to arrive in West Virginia in the 1700s. Later, **settlers** from England and Germany arrived. Over time, these white settlers forced American Indians from their land.

In the 1800s, more Europeans arrived in West Virginia. They came to work on railroads and in coal mines. Many came from countries such as Greece, Hungary, Italy, and Poland.

Today, 91 percent of West Virginians are white. Just under 4 percent are Black. Hispanic and Latino people make up 2 percent of the state's population. About 1 percent of people are Asian. Less than 1 percent are American Indian.

## Culture

Sports are popular in West Virginia. Some football fans root for Marshall University. Others cheer on West Virginia University. Basketball is also popular. West Virginia native Jerry West is one of the greatest basketball players ever.

The logo of the National Basketball Association shows West dribbling a basketball.

Many interesting foods come from West Virginia. In 1927, Italian **immigrant** Giuseppe Argiro sold pepperoni rolls to his friends who worked in the coal mines. Argiro's popular snack became the official food of West Virginia.

## Music in West Virginia

West Virginia is known for its rich musical traditions. Irish and Scottish immigrants brought their traditional songs when they moved to West Virginia in the 1700s. African Americans also introduced blues sounds to the region. The state holds many bluegrass, folk, and blues festivals every year.

Pepperoni rolls are made of bread stuffed with cheese and pepperoni.

The official state fruit of West Virginia is the Golden Delicious apple. The fruit was first grown in the state in 1912. Today, a plaque sits where the original apple tree was planted.

In some places in West Virginia, miners remove the tops of mountains to access coal.

## Industry

West Virginia is one of the top coal producers in the United States. Nearly 13,000 West Virginians work in the coal industry. The state also produces large amounts of oil and natural gas.

Other West Virginians work in **manufacturing**. Goods made in the state include medicines and medical supplies. The company Dow makes chemicals and plastics.

Homer Hickam is a writer and former miner from West Virginia. He talks about what draws people to work as coal miners:

> Every day is an adventure. A lot of folks, their jobs are kind of [boring] and routine, but for coal miners it's not. Every day there's something new.

Source: Michel Martin. "Former Miner Explains the Culture of Mining." *National Public Radio*, 7 Apr. 2010, npr.org. Accessed 27 Nov. 2023.

## What's the Big Idea?

Read this quote carefully. What is its main idea? Explain how the main idea is supported by details.

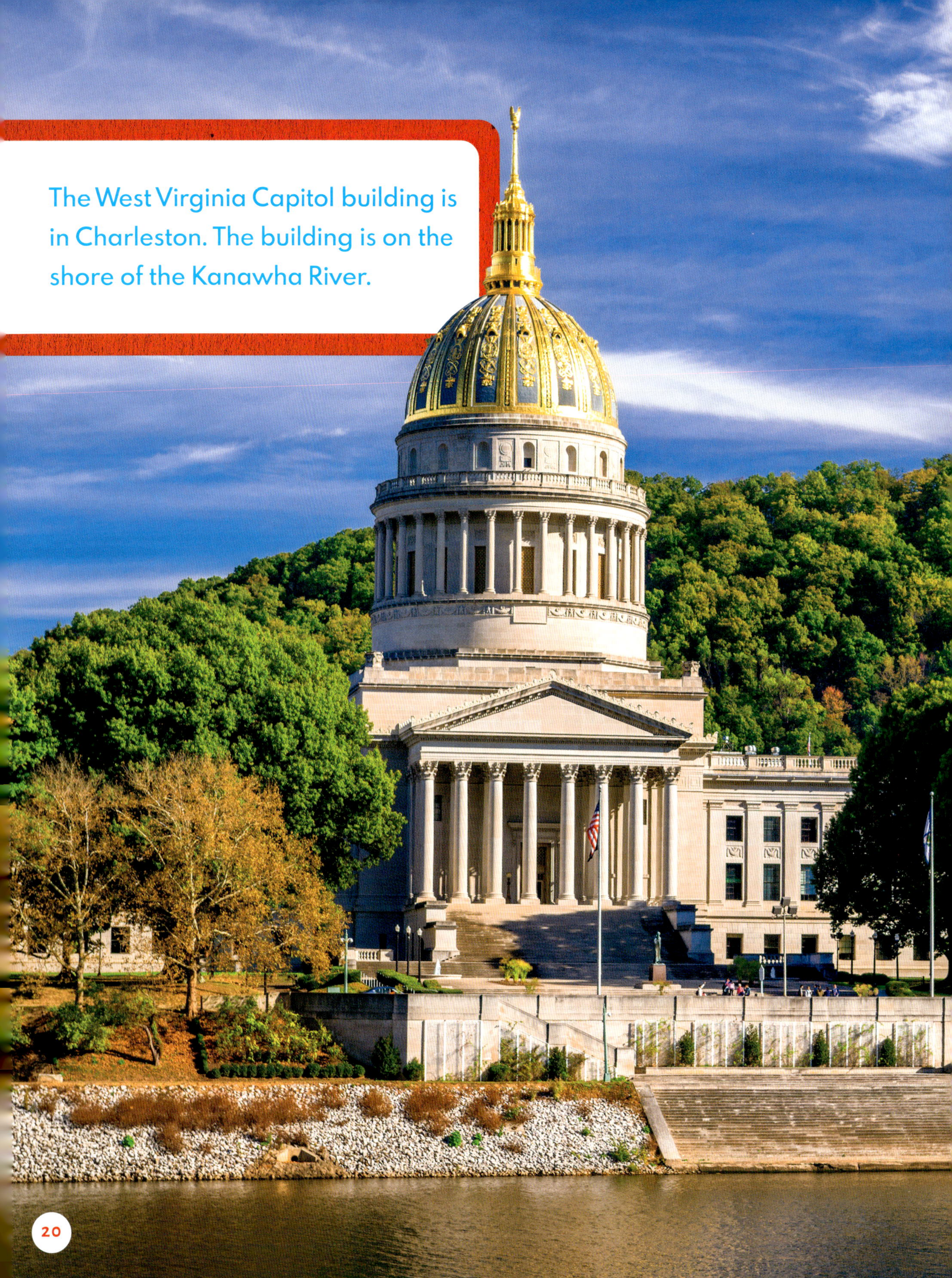

The West Virginia Capitol building is in Charleston. The building is on the shore of the Kanawha River.

# CHAPTER 3

# Places in West Virginia

The capital of West Virginia is Charleston. It is located in the central part of the state. The Clay Center for the Arts and Sciences is a popular museum there. Visitors can explore hands-on exhibits in the Discovery Museum.

Other large cities in West Virginia include Huntington, Parkersburg, Morgantown, and Wheeling.

## Parks

West Virginia has one national park. New River Gorge National Park and Preserve can be found in the southern part of the state. Visitors come to

### The New River Gorge Bridge

New River Gorge National Park and Preserve is famous for its bridge. The New River Gorge Bridge was completed in October 1977. It is the longest steel bridge in North and South America. The bridge is 3,030 feet (924 m) long.

Despite its name, the New River is one of the oldest rivers on Earth.

the park to experience its scenery and to go white water rafting. Many people also like to camp there.

White water rafting is popular in West Virginia. The Gauley River National Recreation Area is one of the most challenging rafting spots in the state. A popular time to go rafting is in September and October. That time of year is known as Gauley Season.

## Landmarks

The Grave Creek Mound Archaeological Complex is in Moundsville. It is the site of a burial mound left by an ancient culture. When the mound was discovered, it was about 70 feet (20 m) tall and 900 feet (275 m) around. Visitors to Grave Creek Mound can view artifacts and **fossils** inside the site's museum.

The Gauley River has five Class V rapids. Class V is one of the most difficult types of rapids for rafting.

The Greenbrier resort covers about 11,000 acres (4,450 ha) of land in southeast West Virginia.

White Sulphur Springs is home to The Greenbrier resort. This historic resort has been open since 1778. The Greenbrier is in the Allegheny Mountains. Many visitors come to the area to see the beautiful views.

There is something for everyone to enjoy in West Virginia. People can go white water rafting or hike through New River Gorge National Park and Preserve. They can learn about the state's history at Grave Creek Mound Archaeological Complex. Or they can try delicious foods from the area. West Virginia is a beautiful place to live and visit.

## Explore Online

Visit the website below. Does it give any new information about West Virginia that wasn't in Chapter Three?

### West Virginia

abdocorelibrary.com/discovering-west-virginia

# State Map

KEY

Capital | Park

City or town | Point of interest

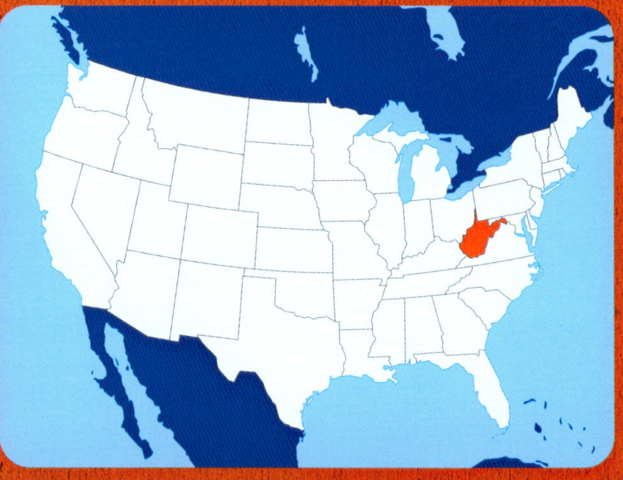

Grave Creek Mound Archaeological Complex

Charleston

# West Virginia: The Mountain State

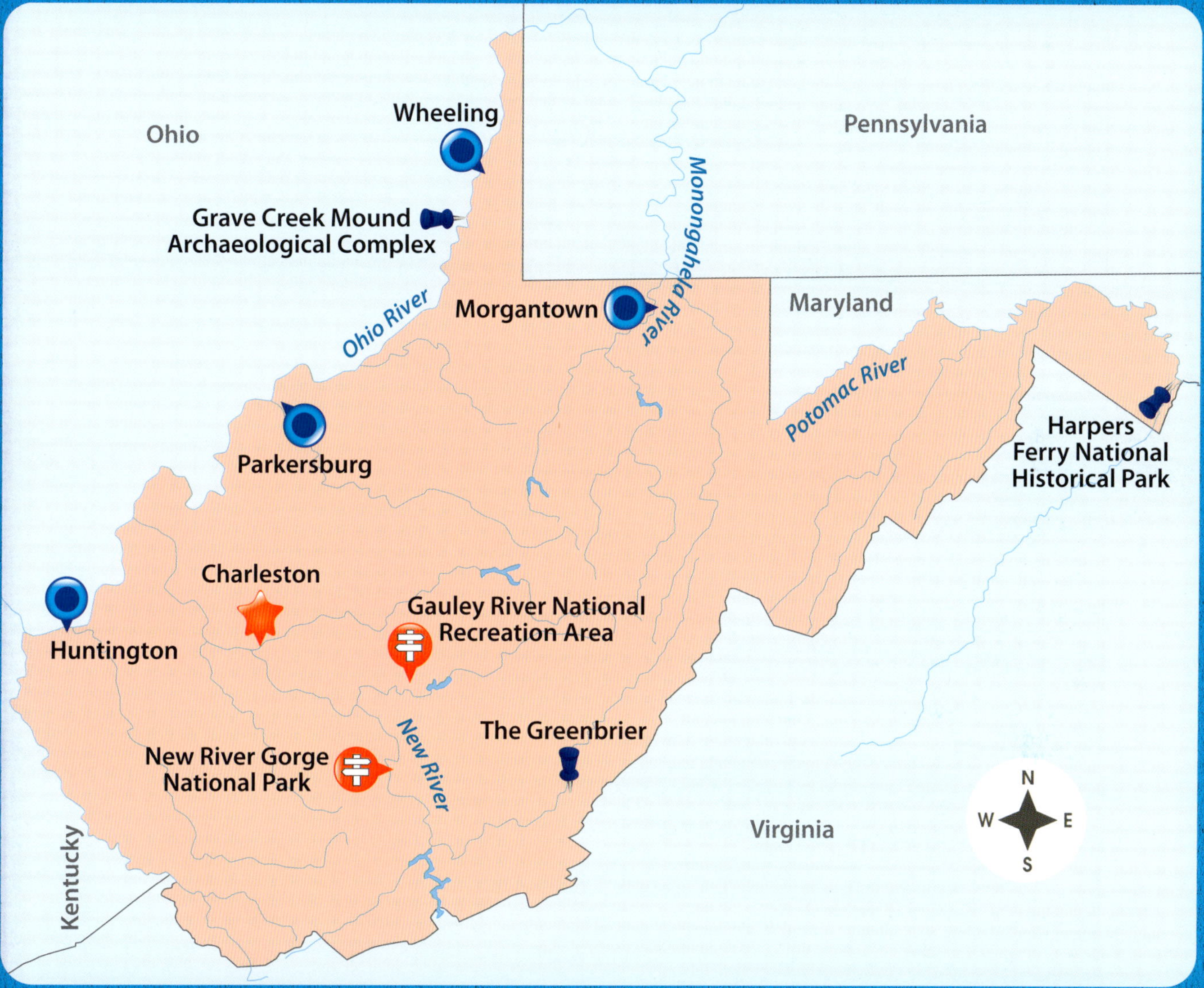

Ohio

Wheeling

Pennsylvania

Grave Creek Mound Archaeological Complex

Monongahela River

Ohio River

Morgantown

Maryland

Potomac River

Parkersburg

Harpers Ferry National Historical Park

Charleston

Gauley River National Recreation Area

Huntington

The Greenbrier

New River Gorge National Park

New River

N

W

E

S

Virginia

Kentucky

Harpers Ferry National Historical Park

# Glossary

**armory**
a building where weapons are kept

**fossils**
the very old, preserved remains of animals or plants

**humid**
describing air that has a lot of moisture

**immigrant**
a person who moves to a different country

**manufacturing**
the process of making goods to sell

**rebellion**
a sometimes violent act that resists authority or the government

**settlers**
people who moved to a new area

**territory**
a particular area of land that belongs to and is governed by a country

# Online Resources

To learn more about West Virginia, visit our free resource websites below.

Visit **abdocorelibrary.com** or scan this QR code for free Common Core resources for teachers and students, including vetted activities, multimedia, and booklinks, for deeper subject comprehension.

Visit **abdobooklinks.com** or scan this QR code for free additional online weblinks for further learning. These links are routinely monitored and updated to provide the most current information available.

# Learn More

Katz, Susan B. *The History of the Civil War*. Rockridge, 2021.

Kavon, Kana. *The 50 States: Amazing Landscapes, Fascinating People, Wonderful Wildlife*. DK, 2021.

Tieck, Sarah. *West Virginia*. Abdo, 2020.

# Index



# About the Author

David J. Clarke is a freelance writer. Originally from Helena, Montana, he now lives in Savannah, Georgia, with his golden retriever, Gus.